STEREOBLIND

Also by Emma Healey

Begin with the End in Mind

STEREOBLIND

POEMS

EMMA HEALEY

ANANSI

Published in Canada in 2018 and the USA in 2018 by House of Anansi Press Inc.
www.houseofanansi.com

House of Anansi Press is committed to protecting our natural environment. As part of our efforts, the interior of this book is printed on paper made from second-growth forests and is acid-free.

22 21 20 19 18   1 2 3 4 5

Library and Archives Canada Cataloguing in Publication

Healey, Emma, 1991–, author
Stereoblind / Emma Healey.

Poems.
Issued in print and electronic formats.
ISBN 978-1-4870-0381-4 (softcover).—ISBN 978-1-4870-0383-8
(PDF)

I. Title.

PS8615.E253S74 2018   C811'.6   C2017-904741-8
C2017-904742-6

Library of Congress Control Number: 2017947367

Book design: Alysia Shewchuk

We acknowledge for their financial support of our publishing program the Canada Council for the Arts, the Ontario Arts Council, and the Government of Canada through the Canada Book Fund.

Printed and bound in Canada

· · · · · · · · ·

Our daughter came out haunted. Right away, we knew. The doctors reached for her but passed their hands through future, half a cloud—weak signal and projection—left her shivering and would not look at us about it. Her right eye floated, flashing, in her head. Stray laughter made her stutter at the edges. Probably we should have been more scared. Our friends would come to visit and we'd be like, *Check it out, somebody tuned the baby between channels.* No one liked that one but us.

Our daughter slept with one eye open, phosphoresced and floating one inch off the mattress. She blew out breakers down the block crying her single, searing pitch. The eye was blue, impossible, and fixed on us. Why were we not more scared? At night, in shifts, we sat alone and watched her watch the dreams that passed across its surface, watched her rise and waver in their swell. The wall-to-wall grew wild beneath our beds, and silence, too, breathed in and out between us. We knew she was deciding. It was time to make our case.

One night, when Michael was out buying groceries, I gathered my courage and the small pile of index cards upon which I had written my notes. In our bedroom, I stood up as straight as I could in the strange light of her, and began my speech. I told her the truth about everything: about the two of us without him, about the debt and guilt and how it never stops. I told our daughter how it felt to fake an orgasm, to cry at lost cat posters until a stranger asks if you're okay, to crave the same aloneness that will kill you. I told her I had long felt shadowed by a terrible sense of premonition, as though my life had been a string of petty crimes I was waiting to be punished for. That, in a sense, I was correct.

Before me our daughter hovered, steady, apparent. I could hear the key in the front door, Michael's shoes on the carpet. I had finished with my notes but could not stop talking. I wanted to make sure I got it all.

STEREOBLIND

FLAT EARTH

Every morning we set up the cameras. Every morning in
dark with the birdsong and buzzsaw we wake and are not
paid enough to build things. Still, we climb and daylight
climbs with us, falls even over everything: the grid, the girls
inside, the snarl of sky, a way to measure time that pulls it
always faster through you. Power lies in definitions—
melting loneliness to aspiration, mystery to physics. There's
the ice that holds the dark that slides rocks boiling
underneath the sidewalk, nights you wake up pinned in
place and choked with want you don't have words for,
spheres that move and sing like honey, right above us and
below. These things are real. We see them on the surface,
step and shine and build new monuments upon them daily,
paid in talking about thinking about seeing, climbing down
to check the cameras. Not enough. It hurts and is a
privilege to know the world for what it truly is, to dream in
sharp relief and wake to darkness, light with all the proof
we have to carry on our own.

Right now, my friend is coming over to meet me. I'm in the kitchen with the radio on, reading, waiting. It's noon, or just past. Spring, some years ago, and warm outside. I'm waiting for him to get here so we can start walking.

In our house, there's always a radio on in each room. They stay tuned to the CBC, out of habit more than preference. From the front door they sound multiple and stuttering, a chorus of ghosts all agreeing on traffic and news *and now the weather forecast for Peterborough and the Kawarthas.* From one room to another they follow you, making you wonder if the sound comes from inside or outside your body.

On the CBC, all the shows have these titles that place you in the present. *Here and Now, Ontario Today.* Once a month they have a gardening show where a guy named Ed takes people's calls about their plants. Right now he's talking to a man with a large spruce. He wants to know if he can prune the tree himself. He's worried about wind. *How big exactly is this tree?* asks Ed, his cadence level, tone bemused. *I can't fit my arms around it,* says the guy.

In my mother's house, the one I grew up in, we did the same thing with the radios. I'd stand in the hallway upstairs, letting the single channel split across me, conducting the pause with my body, transcending the conventions of the instrument.

Right now it's spring. There's a trick you can do with the air and the city and sun that makes your body disappear. My friend doesn't live close to me, but he used to, before I knew him—just blocks away from the house where I live now, inside this poem. Now he lives near where I used to, miles away. One of us is always coming through the past to meet the other where they live.

My friend and I always say we're going to sit and write, but instead we end up walking back and forth, talking about the things we wrote or will have written. *These days*, I tell him sometimes, *I don't know what I sound like.* I want to speak to you with authority, with a sense of purpose third rail underneath my words, but when I try it's like I'm imitating the sound of a language I don't know, just waiting for someone to catch me in the lie.

The last time I wrote poems I was still in school. When someone told me I was good at something I would do it more. I called my book *Begin with the End in Mind*, which is a piece of good advice I stole from someone else's book, a spell about the present with the past and future in it. While I was writing it, someone told me that just because I knew people would like something was not reason enough to write it, and I felt seen for weeks. A curse about the future with the past and present in it.

My friend is writing a poem about repetition, routine. He's tracing his last life all the way across him, through to now. So many things have happened since he moved from here to there; he wants to sort them out. This requires some elision. In his poem, he gets on the streetcar, feels his wallet in the pocket of his jeans, remembers all the other times he's felt it there. In his poem there's no one but him. But here, in the present, in real life, in my poem, you can see it: on the streetcar, he's coming to me.

There's a trick you can do with the radios on in your house
if you pause while you're moving from room to room. The
sound that was ringing the air will start to skip against
itself—constraint, delay. Lately, when people ask what I'm
working on I say, *I'm writing a very elaborate palindrome.* I
want to make something that climbs, pivots, arranges, a
way to work the past against the present and reverse them
both. I want to tell you history is nothing—that sometimes
when you're alone and walking in the city, it could be any
year. I want a pattern I can safely move across, balanced
equation, one clean answer. I won't realize for months
that's not a palindrome at all.

Right now it's still *Ontario Today*, I'm not quite listening, it's just around. The caller's worried that the tree's too big, that it will topple in a storm and wreck his car, come crashing through his bedroom window like a bad dream. *I don't know how I sound*, I say to my friend in this poem or around it, often, walking through the past or to the present, hoping he will tell me. The caller pauses, long. I hear his answer start from the next room before it stutters into this one, just a half-second off.

BAD DREAM

The National Student Loans Service Centre not calling you,
engulfed in flames. Bright, fast, on purpose. Picture
someone running their tongue all the way up your neck
while pinning you to the wall with their free hand. Thirteen
thousand slow miles of telephone cable sparking like stars
at the end, then melting together. A shame. Fourteen floors,
sixteen ghosts, twelve square acres of ill-hidden mirror.
Enough shattered glass. Set apart from its roots and adrift
in the St. Lawrence seaway, declining, a pyre. The horizon.
In the morning in one sense the country will wake and be
lighter by one building. Not you. You'll be pulling its mass
in your lungs, circulation, particular. You will spend all of
your life breathing letterhead in. Old T4s, bills, receipts. All
that proves. Your own balance outstanding. Ontario's air
signed and dated and sharp in your throat when you
swallow. The whole country's reluctant permission enrolled
in your bloodstream, again and again. The National Student
Loans Service Centre may die but knows nothing of death
or escape or consent. You'll assume its ghost daily. Like
prayer. A new organ. To be anxious in all is just more
breathing.

BEAUTIFUL BOYS

Pink silk jackets. Feathered hair, impeccable skateboards, liquid jawlines, triplicate. Thin hands gripping thin forearms, in a pyramid in order the Beautiful Boys doppling down your street like a snake, or the dream you had about a snake. Taken together they sing like distant pavement in a heat wave, colour warbling at the edges like a melted vhs, craft beer dying in the backs of all their throats like a bad secret. Eyes like wrenches. Skin like petals. Wheels that whisper to the pavement as they pass under your window: *please yes please yes please yes please*

After we talked I started reading this article called *Can the Bacteria in Your Gut Explain Your Mood?* I've always been interested in the different ways in which I am responsible for my own sadness. *Changing a patient's bacteria,* the article said, *might be difficult, but it still seemed more straightforward than altering his genes.*

Laboratory mice, said the article, *were dropped into tall, cylindrical columns of water in what is known as a forced-swim test, which measures over six minutes how long the mice swim before they realize that they can neither touch the bottom nor climb out, and instead collapse into a forlorn float. Researchers use the amount of time a mouse floats as a way to measure what they call "behavioral despair."*[1]

1   *(Antidepressant drugs, like Zoloft and Prozac, were initially tested using this forced-swim test.)*

The pills I take every morning are packaged and sold under the brand name Wellbutrin. Their main ingredient is a chemical called bupropion, which is built to linger in your blood like a bad dream for days after you take it. This way you can skip a day, as I often do, out of forgetfulness, and feel no major changes in your body or your brain.

People will tell you the drugs themselves are not enough to fix things. To be normal, you need goals, routine. Something to hold you down. On the phone, we'd been making a list: stay busy. Make your mind blank. Lists. Exercise. Don't obsess. Have control. Let things happen. Be kind, forgiving. Don't get pushed around. Sleep enough but not too much. Don't do drugs but do the right ones. Don't drink. Quit your context. Stick it out. Be social. Don't slide. Be open, always changing, but stay fixed in place and someday you'll hit a clear patch, fall in sync with the machine, love and be loved and be able to contain it, care for real about the outcome. Exercise, eat salad, take the time you need for you, check in about your motivations and your needs, respect yourself while pushing past your limits, kale, hydration, trips to see the doctor, new machines at the gym, telling your friends when you need help or time alone, listen without hearing only your own voice in your head, chasing after the right people with the right qualities for the right reasons, pinning some girl to the mattress or the hardwood, arms above her head, because she asked you and you trust me when I say that's how I want it, believing other people when they say they want you. One day you'll wake up and the world will be there and you'll want it. Honest and clear and just one way, the good one. Promise.

There's a trick you can do with your body if there's someone who's willing to help you. Get them to lie flat on their stomach, then lie on top of them, facing down. Spread your weight out as evenly as possible, no tensing. Then just lie there, still as you can, and float along the small of both your breathing. If you do this right, after a few minutes it's like the other person isn't there at all.

We were talking, I think, on the phone, about gesture, resolution. I can't remember now who was saying what but we agreed that the most tiring part is not doing the thing, or how often it feels fraudulent and empty. The real exhaustion, we agreed, comes from losing track. Your focus slips from the task at hand—pressing into my wrists with your thumbs, washing that dish and then the next one— and for a second you see the shape of your life already, if you're lucky. You see its rising line and lift and downward slope, and then you see yourself doing it over and over and over with no end until it stops, I said, my shoulders pressed against the sheets, alone, to you. One of us laughed. Then the other.

The article was pages long, comprehensive in its research, optimistic in its turn. The forced swim thing was just a few sentences, a speed bump on the way to a larger point. The cylinders are tall and wide enough that the mice, once inside, cannot escape on their own. The test measures over six minutes how long they swim before they realize that they can neither touch the bottom nor climb out. They can tell the drugs are working if the mice keep swimming. By the time I'd finished reading it was too late to call you again.

The catch is that if one of you moves, the whole thing pins itself backwards, and your awareness switches course. Suddenly, you've never been more clearly one of two people. A body touched at all points by another.

The drugs you take have a much shorter half-life than mine, fifteen hours or so. This might be why, when we have sex, it comes on for each of us as it does: for me, a long electric draw, and for you, a switch, flipping. For both of us, it's violent: I kiss you and you push me, I move and you pin me in place, etc.

On the phone, we agreed about playing the small range of gestures again and again. Some days you meet yourself staring at the bottle of pills, or the jagged corner of a dish that's somehow been shattered in the sink, or the uneven eyes of a young woman who has her own reasons for wanting to feel the full weight of your anger, and you don't want to stop, but you don't want to keep going either. So what do you do?

Sometimes the question of what is made inside or outside the body feels pressing. I'll be out in the world by myself, among others—at the gym, running on the treadmill, or in the grocery store, staring up at a punishing multiplicity of hummus—and all of a sudden I know something endless and dark wants its way through me, wants to take my bones out one by one, to swallow and dissolve. In these moments, the world drops away and I stand there forever—my face strange, my fists tiny and strange— sweating under the fluorescents. In these moments, I can feel the things it's already claimed, aching just outside my reach, like phantom limbs.

We were talking about nothing, how it changes all the time. I never say this, but when I let you pin me down I'm trying to teach you something about ownership, desire, intent and gesture, repetition, being inside, outside, both, alone. Permission. When we talk sometimes I feel you testing me for weak spots, and I know you're scared—of me, and all the things you think I mean you want and might not have or get to. I know how this ends already, and what fear will make you do to me, and how you'll make it stop. I didn't say, I know exactly what will happen. It's a symptom of the thing I take the pills for.

Picture a man in a pharmaceutical research facility. He's standing behind a thick pane of two-way glass, in a white room, wearing a clean white coat. It's springtime, early afternoon. There's just one window open. A lone car alarm, blocks away, drifts in, pulsing, *forlorn float*. Outside, his colleagues are waiting with their clipboards. The man is still, poised over an array of glass cylinders, each identical in shape and volume. His arms are lifted. The world stays still. He waits, like a member of the orchestra, for his cue.

Is this the machine where we're supposed to put that
feeling? Or what? I can't stop saying *at the level of the
gesture*, but fuck if I know, everyone's holding a fish. Or a
puppy. They just told me, *put it here, say what's about you,
start deciding*. So: semaphore, a trailing school of shirtless
ghosts all *hey/yeah/haha/you* into your hipbones in a round.
You have to ring like something's struck you every time, it's
just and sucks to ask yourself what loneliness you tried to
skip and got here. Plus the world in its new order coils
against your dumb potential. Thinned to channels. Twinned
and faultless. Your desire. Some relief. All gesture claws a
canyon up your ribcage now and *by yourself* means *like
conducting*. Like, as in the opposite of no. Don't look again:
that's you, bright signal in among the noise and you, a
steady please unfolding in the wireless. Sing it again, alone
for once for real. Say how it sounds to want to ache and to
be counted.

At first I liked the test because I couldn't tell what made the
questions like each other. It's sexy to be led to someone
else's revelation, so I was pretty disappointed when I got
there on my own: it was just empathy and violence, like
everything else is. *I already know what kind of person I am*, I
could have told the guy as he was setting up the screens,
but chickened out at the last second. Each time I breathed a
wash of golden pixels, each time I spoke it scrolled out icy
'80s Tandy blue. One of the questions was about my
mother.

I'll tell you about my mother: when I was twenty years old I
couldn't afford a bicycle, so she went to the bike guy and
picked one out for me—a vintage Raleigh, orange. She
rode it around the field behind his house to test the brakes,
then put it in her car and drove it all the way to Montreal,
where the ceiling in my terrible apartment was buckling in
slow, beautiful waves. It was like sleeping underneath a
dream about the ocean that could kill you in real life, but it
had always been that way—the only thing connecting any
room to any other was the fact that we could pass between
them. When we moved in we'd found the bathroom door
hidden underneath a pile of empties in the backyard, and
once my mom went home that's where I locked and never
rode the gift she'd brought me. I was scared. What else is
new? I'd go down, gaze into the shards and see myself
thrown into traffic, sidewalk singing in my knees, hot
chrome between my teeth, etc. *That pupil doesn't dilate*, I

tried to tell the guy as he adjusted his big leather pedal, *it's a whole thing*, but he kept trying to make it work.

I wanted to ask him whether he thought that story was about guilt or clarity or debt, whether he felt that in a sense we were both working toward the same ultimate goal. I wanted to explain that in the '90s it was hard to touch a person without failing just a little, and that just as some things live inside you without showing on the surface, there are memories you bear the sign of on your body without ever having seen in full. But he didn't want to hear it. He was busy with his work.

Emma is home alone and leaves the water running. Then she falls asleep. It slips across the floor, down through the walls, and into Sam's apartment like summer rain, so gentle that at first he doesn't even notice. A pattern spreads across the ceiling, like the scars a lightning strike can leave on skin. Our landlord will tell us there's no real damage, but some nights, flicking a light switch, you can hear a chorus in the walls that doubles, triples, waves as if it's rising from the sea.

Layne is home alone and falls asleep. Wakes up with a start.
Two raccoons are pressed up against her window, looking
in. Eyes glowing, moonlight-tipped fur, paws uncanny —
they don't move for Layne, now doubled over, breathing in
her bed. Time is frozen in the room, but out on Parkside,
cars still move. Their headlights throw twin shadows on her
wall.

I'm home alone, can't sleep.[2] I check the back lock, close
the window in my bedroom, pull the baby gate across the
stairs to keep the dog in, double-check the front door as I
leave. The sky this summer seems to belong to somewhere
else. At dusk, you wonder what unfortunate desert town
has accidentally picked up the Toronto sky. Whose citizens
feel crowded, claustrophobic, can't think why.

When I arrive back home, the dog is somehow standing on
the bright green lawn, staring up at the full moon, panting
quietly. This is the stillest I have ever seen him, and yet he
gives the impression of being propelled forward into some
great unknown, like the figurehead on the prow of an
ancient ship.

---

2   Sam dreams of wrestling the landlord, a dream he may have
inherited from previous tenants. The landlord wants to fight. He
has a key to the side door. Sam asks him to leave but it's too late,
so he takes the landlord out, with tenderness, into the driveway,
and brings him down to the ground. They stay that way, locked
together, crying, then not crying anymore.

Months later, we're preparing an elaborate meal. It's three days before Christmas. Emma is in the kitchen making breakfast cocktails, Sam and Layne are in the living room building a UFO out of gingerbread. I am lying on my stomach on the kitchen floor, staring into the eyes of the dog, trying as always to find out if he loves me.

I look up, and there's the landlord, standing at the mouth of our kitchen, a trail of fresh slush glistening behind. With him is a young man none of us have seen before, holding a tripod twice his size, arms trembling with the effort. *Who are you?* our landlord asks me. Before I have the chance to answer, he tells us.

Our house begins each day in silence; by the end it's a riot of traffic and weather. Every room has a radio in it. Emma likes to switch each one on as she moves through the house, but she doesn't switch them off again. Today, I follow, turning off whatever she turns on. We move through the house in this way all afternoon, trailing sound and light behind us, two waves that crest and split and merge again, in mourning.

*Wake Up Sunday Morning In Your Recently Renovated Abode,
Throw Up The Sash, Take A Deep Cleansing Breath Of
Morning Air As You Gaze Over At High Park. The Kids
Slowly Open Your Bedroom Door And Ask Are You Ready Yet?
Your Front Door Is Less Than 100 Yards To The Main
Entrance Of The Park. Your Answer Is Yes, But Shhhh, Don't
Wake Up Mom Then Out You Go, Alone Time With Your
Kids. The Sky Is Aqua Blue, The Birds Are Chirping And The
Flowers Are Blooming.*

*Then It's Back Home For Sunday Morning Brunch In Your
Lavish Family Kitchen, Don't Forget That Perfect Pot Of Coffee
With Your Sunday Morning Paper, Just You, Your Partner
And The Light Breeze Off The Lake—Now This Is It!*

Layne is working on something at Ontario Place. She's learning about how the city operates. *Did you know you can buy rights to the air?* she asks me.

She says Ontario Place is built on landfill, that they took debris from old, demolished buildings and dumped it in the water in the night and no one stopped them. She says the people from the city and the people from the province can't decide who owns the islands. She says the word *Ontario* has to do with the lake. She says the people who buy the right to say they own the air from the people who say they own the city get to decide what kinds of glass or light or words go in it. Everybody thinks they own the water, but we can see it from our front yard—it just keeps rising, every day.

I'm trying so hard to write a poem about the differences
between things, how they disappear. It's my only job and
I'm failing. I want to write something you can read
forwards and backwards, that looks the same way both
ways, builds meaning by crossing itself from itself. I want
to write about Paul and John and what happens when
someone pins you into a poem, about Mathew and Alex
and trading your life for someone else's, about Craig
strobing in and out of my life, about why women never end
up in the work even though it only exists because of them.
I want to lay my life out in clean lines, to show you how
good I am at leaving nothing undone, touching right wire
to right wire, lighting it up. A solved equation with my self
erased completely. I want to deliver the answer to me across
time and come out lighter. But every time I write, it sounds
like wringing apology from my own throat.

The real estate agent plants his sign in our lawn like a flag, takes a key. His business is called YOUR WAY OUT; the phrase is stamped across his face in screaming red.

One day, a pile of business cards appears upon the counter. The next, a few are fixed to the fridge. The cards are laminated, in case someone tries to set them on fire. For weeks, we find them everywhere: stacked in the cabinets, clogging the shower drain. The dog coughs and a few flutter out of his mouth, lightly chewed.

One night before bed, I lift my pillow and find one where I usually keep a crystal to cleanse my dreams. The real estate agent's gleaming white teeth are arranged in a neat, endless row, like piano keys in a nightmare.

First-time buyers begin to appear. In daylight, they wander in and out of our house, pointing out flaws. *What are you doing?* a couple asks, twin shadows in the doorway of my bedroom. *I am failing at my job,* I tell them. *Oh.* Others move toward my window in drifts, inspecting the hole in the glass, troubling the weak border between this room and the next. You can't blame someone for wanting to be safe. No one has forced us to write poetry, or dance, or curate bicycle tours that bring people to different site-specific artworks in the summer. It's not a crime to have millions of dollars, or people in your life who will lend you millions of dollars.

Still, some of them lower their eyes, a little sorry. Time progresses. They multiply. We stop locking the door, stop looking up when they enter. We become attendants in the museum of us. They pass through our rooms while we shower, have sex. Some will ask, flipping over a couch cushion or moving a few plates aside to inspect the hedgehog-themed kitchen tiles, if we are sad to have to leave. They keep their shoes on. It's no one's fault.

In the living room, they squint at the objects on our shelves—some foreign magazines, a 3D-printed model of the dog, twenty YOUR WAY OUT cards caught in a bell jar. One woman asks me whether all these things are art. I tell her they're the kinds of things you own when you cannot control your future.

I have this feeling Sam and Layne were in love once. No proof, just a thought. *Have you ever actually seen his place?* she asks me.[3]

She asks if I've ever had the new-room dream. *People in packed cities get it all the time,* she says, *this dream where they open up a closet door and find a whole new wing of their house inside.* She says she has it every night.

Sam's kitchen table is covered with pieces of broken mirror, camera lenses scattered everywhere. There's one very small door set at a strange angle against the kitchen's back wall. She leads me through it, down a set of stairs then up another, into a bedroom that seems somehow to be both floating above the ground and buried underneath it. Weak light filters in through the low windows.

---

3   Sam has one job—which is to take things out of the back of his truck and then put them back in again—and one hobby, which is kite surfing. I do not know what kite surfing is, but one night I ask him what he likes about it, and the sweet light of the world seems to bend around him. In love and reminded, relieved, he gazes into the middle distance. *I don't mean to sound like a pagan,* he says, *but once you're out there, you're just ... holding hands with the wind.*

I have a hangover. It's a Sunday in the floating months; outside, there's a blizzard. My whole face throbs around my blazing right eye. The dog is impatient with me. I wrap myself in scarves and step out onto the porch. The city is frozen and gleaming and silent.

Two hours later I am somehow in the glittering heart of it, inside a Bed Bath & Beyond. I have been carried there by a force stronger than my will, one I am powerless to question. There are no other customers in the Bed Bath & Beyond. It seems empty of staff, too, even though I know they're embedded somewhere in its landscape, eyes flashing, still among the stacks of non-stick cookware, waiting for me to form a question.

It's wonderful inside the Bed Bath & Beyond. The fluorescence is flat with a cruel edge; I feel alert but not ugly, every object piled from floor to ceiling has the same dull sheen. In the water section, I stand below a shelf three times my height, stare up at all the things I could use to carbonate liquids in my own home. It's a thrill to be alive in such a world, where every problem has a multiplicity of solutions, one honest light spread evenly across them.

Our landlord[4] drives a disappearing Lamborghini. Each time we see it, the rust has claimed more ground. The car is crumpled on one side, as though someone once drove it into a wall, then just kept driving.

---

4   He cannot tell the three of us apart. The past splits open for him, too. It's important to acknowledge this. Indistinguishable, we multiply in front of him: me and Emma, Emma and Layne and me. Each time he returns to the house there are more of us, dressed in black, agreeing. He dreams of us forcing him to chew on our hair. This place was his and now it's full of women. That's important to remember.

One day, his brother[5] follows in a very large truck. Together, in the bleak mid-morning light, they lean a ladder up against the shed and begin the complex ritual of removing years' worth of garbage from its roof. There are many inexplicable poles. The brothers tie them loosely to the U-Haul in a way that demonstrates great faith in the universe but a poor understanding of physics. More than once, our landlord wanders too close to the edge of the roof and looks down suddenly, as though startled from a deep sleep.

Out of nowhere, Layne appears behind me, sipping coffee from a mug that bears the words "TENNESSEE: THE VOLUNTEER STATE." She joins me at the window. *Do you think we're going to watch them die?* she asks.

---

5   Our landlord dreams of his wife, surrounded by globes that glow from the inside. She's smashing each one with a hammer. She's dropping a lit cigarette on my bedroom's hardwood floor, grinding it in with the heel of her boot. He watches, does nothing to stop her. The building lights up from the inside. Just in time, he snaps out of it, smashes my window, climbs out along a rotting lattice, hoping it will hold.

Our landlord owns a tool belt that holds two bottles of beer, one for each hip. One day, wheeling my bike into the backyard, I see him in the lawn chair he unloads each day from the trunk of his car, addressing a rat that has ventured onto our property. *Are you a good mouse or a bad mouse?* he asks, unlit cigarette dangling from his lips. A note of startling tenderness spreads through the question like a sunrise. He pulls a half-empty 50 from his belt and salutes the rat in a gesture of solidarity.

One day, there are no more first-time buyers. The next, too, the door stays locked. On the third, I feel a text message shiver through the house: Emma's phone upstairs, Layne's in the kitchen, Sam's outside on the hood of his truck. The message reads: *191 Parkside is no longer for sale.*

We all rush to the front window. The real estate agent is grimly unstaking his face from the lawn. He throws it into the back seat of his car, trailing clods of dirt.

The next two months proceed in a complex silence. It's dangerous to want, to fix, to ask. We are passing through the eye.

Alone, I blow a breaker with the toaster, send myself
downstairs to reset it.

The basement is dark and rough and endless as the
basement in a horror film. At the end of one unlit corridor,
I see a light on. There's a single furnished room. Inside,
the floor is brand-new hardwood. There's a single bed, a
folding table, a boom box with no tape inside. Along the
opposite wall sits a beautiful fireplace. Inexplicably, there is
a fire there, lit and roaring.

Next to the breaker panel sits a framed cartoon of a cow,
with the words "ART MOO-VEAU" underneath it. Gently, I
remove the picture from the wall and carry it with me
upstairs, set it across from me on my bed, and stare at it
for an hour, unsure what kind of crime I've just committed.

Sam says something about the black mould downstairs. *Yeah, dude,* he says, *all over, probably. You guys don't see it?* He notices my face and rushes to repair things. *You haven't lived here long enough. You don't have to worry about it. I might have to worry a little bit.*

I'm still trying to write my way out. I make notes about the organ, about pills and value and fucking. I cut pages out of emails and other people's books and lay them on the floor, move the pieces around like a detective tracking a killer. I step over the mess of my answer every night on my way to bed, until one day the dog finally steps on it too, and chews, and sleeps, and I feel a great, crushing relief.

One day in the winter good weather arrives, along with a
package from Carlo, all the way from the other side of the
country. False spring, or the promise of a real one, breathes
through the hole in my window. I am lit up with purpose.

Inside the package, there's a tape. The first song is a
woman singing in a church. Her voice is laced with static;
behind her, a piano thunders like a wave crashing down on
a sunlit beach, or the happiest person in the world
throwing a piano down the stairs. A chorus rises around
her; their breathing is ragged. They have travelled across
time to reach me here. *Makes me glad*, they yell. *Makes me
glad makes me glad makes me glad.* It's the warmest sound
I've ever heard.

Listen: there are all kinds of people in this poem, walking
around, turning lights on, wincing at the cold wind, saying
no. But Carlo is at the end of it, waiting for me.

Spring comes.

A float of plastic butterflies appears in the front yard.

At first, we don't know who put them there. You just walk out of the house and there's this swarm of pink and purple, stuck into the lawn with thin stakes.

We begin keeping watch. She comes in the dead of night or dawn, wearing an enormous hat, rearranging the butterflies, complicating their order unnecessarily. Her nervous energy reminds me of something I'd rather not think about. The van she drives has the words A WOMAN'S TOUCH printed along the side, in searing pink.

Next, two men arrive in a different van with an enormous, life-sized portrait of them on the side. *A father-son business,* Sam suggests to one of them, making conversation. *Uncle-nephew,* the nephew says.

In the photo on their van they're wearing the coveralls they wear every day, and smiling. On breaks, they slouch against their double portrait, scowling and smoking in tandem. A reflection, photonegative.

Sam buys an enormous tent that attaches permanently to the roof of his truck. *So you can go anywhere, sleep wherever,* he says to me. I haven't seen Layne in weeks.

The uncle smokes blunts with one hand, builds an enormous scaffolding around our house with the other. The things they do make our house shake. They start at dawn, stay until eight or nine, peer through our windows. Once, I hear the nephew ask the uncle how old he thinks we are. *Gotta be careful,* he says. They both laugh.

For months, they sit shoeless on the scaffolding, discussing the shape of the earth. There's a plexiglass dome over its surface, they agree, and an enormous ice wall that rings it to keep the oceans in. *Who protects the ice wall from explorers?* I ask. NASA, the uncle says. What about gravity? I ask. *Imagine a car,* the nephew tells me, so I do. *Now imagine if that car just kept speeding up forever.*

The first-time buyers return. This time they're men alone in suits that smell like plaster dust and money. They move through our home in a cloud of renovation, ball their fists at all the bowing glass, ready to strike the first blow.

I go to get my tarot cards read. The woman doing the reading is also an artist who makes feminist weavings. She fixes me with a look that makes me feel like I'm on fire. Her one-eyed pug sits next to her, gazing into my one eye. It knows. The artist draws my cards and says, *I am not in the habit of giving advice but you need to get out of wherever you're living.* I look to the pug for guidance but she is now, somehow, all the way across the room.

The artist writes my reading down on a thin piece of notebook paper, but as I'm walking out, clouds blacken and the sky opens up. By the time I get home the note is soaked, bleeding into itself, impossible to read.

For weeks I bike and sweat between the city's smallest places, breathing in centuries of dust, trying to imagine a future underground. One day, on my way home, a pack of teenage boys assembles behind me. They trail me for blocks, under the overpass, into the brilliant sunset. Some bike in front, some follow behind, breaking apart around me and reforming like a flock of birds in flight. *Do your mothers know where you are?* I ask, and they just laugh and laugh and laugh and laugh and laugh.

I go to a party in an abandoned condo sales centre.[6]
Someone has wrapped all the showroom furniture in white
vinyl. It looks like the end of the world. There's a river of
translucent blue plastic crystals running through the
building's lobby. They look real, like they spent centuries
forming in the earth. I dip my hand in to take one, but a
woman appears behind me. *If everyone did that*, she says,
there wouldn't be any crystals left.

---

6   I bike home along the water, watching all the mirrored glass
show the lake to the lake. The water keeps rising. That night, I
dream it comes up so high it pours through the hole in my
window, thin shards of mirror floating on its surface.

Layne invites me to come see her new art project. She's built a whole new city in Ontario Place. Its theme is the future, how it skips into the present. It happens in the weather pavilions, inside the now-overgrown log flume, in the Visitors' Centre. They've strung lights across areas where school groups used to congregate, are screening old government propaganda in the Cinesphere. By the lake, a video of a woman swimming is projected onto a translucent screen, so that the image of water and the water behind it seem to merge and split. By the edge of the island, a woman dances alone on a breaker, her scarves flying into the sunset. Inside one of the silos, a friend of Layne's has built a tornado. We all sit underneath it with our legs crossed; it whispers to us in a child's voice.

Everywhere in this city of the future, people walk arm in arm, discussing their childhoods. Along the beach, the sound of a different beach, busier than this one, is broadcast over the loudspeakers that once played park announcements. On the water, a man sits in the province's last remaining swan boat, playing a mournful song on the trumpet while two civilians paddle him around the perimeter.

Joyful, confused and overcome, I rest under a false cliff, below the log flume. Above me, a pine tree rotates slowly, spotlit. Nearby, I find a plaque: *Choreographed to pause briefly*, it says, *confounding expectations of typical tree behaviour, the tree periodically seems to rejoin the living world.*

Back home, standing on the front porch, I hear someone breathing. It's Sam. He's sitting up on the scaffolding piled up around our house. His silhouette is pitched against the holographic moon. He's smiling, holding hands with the wind.

They sell the house. This is Emma's story to tell, not mine. She comes home and the landlord and the buyers are sitting in the front yard in a cloud of plastic butterflies, drinking cheap sparkling wine. They invite her to join them, seem relieved when she declines.

On the last day of the summer, in her city on the island, Layne lets me ride in the swan boat. I wear a wedding dress and take passengers, three at a time, into the tunnel of love. I read them poems about the radio, poems about walking. The sound of my voice doubles, bounces off the walls. I've been trying for so long to say what I mean about time, but still can't pin the truth of it in place. I tell people it feels like a stack of transparencies, all printed with the same picture, layered overtop each other, slipping apart, out of order. My voice crests and floats and breaks against the walls. Waves come in from the lake, are gentle by the time they reach us. The swan's beak nudges the ceiling of the tunnel. A larger truth is beginning to reveal itself, in the corners, but I still can't see it yet.

In this scene it's night, like always. Our hero stares down at a handful of old photographs, picks at the keyboard, maybe dreams about a unicorn, etc. Around her, broken lamps, spent pens, piles of small crystals, pill jars, camera lenses, unlit candles, notebook paper, half-wound tapes, full ashtrays, record sleeves, all the kinds of glass that happen when a person lives alone. The sink behind her out of focus, piled with dishes, kitchen floor in black and white, small pattern that gets bigger as we move toward the centre of the image. That's perspective. Light from the crowded world outside melts through the room behind her, on her knees before the screen, where we can see displayed a wash of static and the grid, which never changes, plus the faces of some people we don't know. Still, we understand the greater meaning: *shards refusing to make a pattern, tiny mirror that fails to focus in small the whole of the great room.* We know, too, without needing to be told that while some people might be born to be with others, others still are built to spend their nights like this, tracking a past that isn't theirs with antique, glitching equipment. Which kind are you? *Stop, enhance.* Small trail of symbols, significance of the bicycle, all this glowing and pause. A dull roar rushes through the room, subsides. She looks good, caught up, flickering inside the question, almost there but not there yet.

ADDERALL

Above or underground you're second person, sorry. Still
again like sex you pull it through you without thinking, let
the gold guilt echo glitter through your pulse for hours.
Still, you can't stop. Sorry. Count it again: her laugh, his
eyes, their arms, at home, at parties, propped up on your
elbows doing laundry, *how she touched me, how he sounded
when he slept*, pressed up against the bar, palm-first against
the podium, a crowd of you. No climb, no trying, glass-edged
stutter, double flash of half-life in your speech. Stay still, so
still you start to shiver. Cheek against the hardwood. Keep
your mouth closed. Clean. We know you like this, finally in
order: paper plane, jet engine, a machine like any other.
Run it back.

At work, we watch a video of a deaf woman doing chores.
The man who loves her is named Possum; he is either a
possum or a man dressed in a possum costume. Possum
and the woman communicate via elegant and careful
gestures, two voice-overs filling the space between them.

Possum's fur is filthy. His nose is black, as if someone has
coloured it in with a marker. Many things are unclear: does
he live with the woman? Are they in love? Her hobbies are
cleaning the kitchen and stamping paper very carefully with
a piece of triangular foam dipped in pink paint. Sometimes
Possum tries to help her. He is taller but knows less about
the world. Sometimes their friend, a beautiful woman who
never smiles, stops by to drop off a pair of homemade
stilts.

One weekend, the woman goes out of town to visit a friend.
It's Possum's job to take care of the garden and make sure
the house stays neat, but he misses the woman so much he
decides to ride out her absence in a deep sleep, make the
days disappear.

He falls asleep in the garden in a beam of pure sunshine,
but when he wakes up several hours later, he is under the
mistaken impression a whole day has passed. Does Possum
not understand time because he is a child, or because he is
a man, or because he is a possum, or because he is in love?

There's no clear answer; he repeats the gesture again and again.

Single as Penelope, Possum paces the garden, staring up into a cloudless sky, trying to change time and how it moves, signing to himself and to me, though he does not know I'm there. As night falls on the second day, which by his metric is the ninth, he sits under a tree in the empty garden, lists all the things he loves about the woman. As he does this—her red hair, her generosity, her fastidiousness with the paint—the video cuts, briefly, to an image of two hands in an otherwise empty room, slowly signing the word *l o n e l y*, teaching us how to say it in his language.

Eventually his beloved returns. Possum rushes into her arms. *You were gone for nine whole days!* he signs. *Oh, Possum,* she says, *you're so silly, it was only a weekend.* Her voice is tender, but she's squinting, holding him by his shoulders at arms' length. If she asks him what he means, the sky will splinter into pieces, the earth will shake and open up and swallow him. "Oh ..." he signs, hands drifting in the air. Before she can tell him anything, the screen flashes back to a pair of hands. Letter by letter, they spell out the word *a l o n e*.

There were twelve of us, in total, in the study, but everyone had the same problem: money moved into and out of our lives like air. I'd been working nights at the university, pretending to be sick so that students could pretend to figure out what was wrong with me. I was always pregnant or suicidal. For hours I'd sit, legs dangling off the side of the exam table, shoulders torqued forward from the weight of my fictional burden, thin hospital paper tearing underneath me when I moved. My supervisor told me not to make direct eye contact with the students, who all looked like people I'd gone to high school with. Every ten minutes, I whispered my lines to the floor: *I don't know what I'm going to do. Will you have to call my parents?* Behind the two-way glass, professors stood, evaluating our performances.

At the end of every shift I'd emerge from the ancient mouth of the university, blinking its darkness back, turning from the woman I'd been all day for money into the one I was outside, alone, for free. In these moments, the world seemed held together at strange angles.[7] Past and present flickered out of order like the picture in a kicked TV.

---

7   One morning, riding the streetcar home, I saw a man I recognized leaning against a bus shelter, talking to a woman I didn't know. Months earlier, after a party, this guy had sent me a message to ask if a friend of mine was single. *I don't normally do this*, he wrote, *but this time I have to*. Another time, I watched a woman cry about him in a bar. *He's a really nice person,* she told me. A third, I was standing in a small, crowded room next to a friend and watched him walk toward us. When he placed his hand on her wrist I felt the current pass between them, like it was also meant to pass through me.

Watching from the streetcar this time, I saw he didn't see me. Against the tempered glass he seemed to glow from the inside: sleeves rolled up, hands in his pockets, ankles crossed, jaw clenched, swipe of pink light licking up his throat. I watched him until we moved again, rode home shot through with a fear I couldn't place or name or lose for days.

Things weren't the worst they'd ever been. I washed dishes and took my pills. In the mornings I did stretches in front of an enormous prescription lamp that was supposed to blast happiness into me through my pores. Outside, above ground, the subway rushed past my house on its silver track, screaming an amazing chord of light and air and metal.

It was like running up a down escalator. I'd forget one of my senses for weeks until the world gave it back to me. I read a lot of books, I phoned my mother and my grandmother. Time pulled me under like a wave, or I could feel it pressing me flat into half of myself. Sometimes repetition felt like prayer. Others, even ten minutes of silence could kill me.

Some days I'd wake up and know I'd landed too close to the third rail. My hands would be half-disappeared, like in the photo from *Back to the Future*, or I'd have bruises, as though someone had cracked my ribcage open in the night and installed a whole new universe inside me. Sometimes I felt a loose alliance with myself: two idiots walking around, bumping into things. Some days I was so lonely that the sound of my own breathing made me gag. In my dreams, there was violence more elaborate than anything I'd ever seen awake: deep, sharp, red, everywhere. I didn't know how my brain could assemble so many new kinds of horror. I wondered if it meant I still knew how to make things.

One night, at Sarah's place, I started shaking and could not stop. We'd been smoking weed and looking at pictures of ALF on her computer. Through the thin walls, I could hear her neighbour having sex. I wanted to tell her the thing about time, how it kept doubling back across me, but I thought it might freak her out. Instead I got up, called a cab and slowly drank a glass of water while she watched me from the couch, worried.

When I climbed into the car, the driver told me he'd just seen a coyote run across the road. *Have you noticed all the coyotes?* he said. *They're everywhere.* With one hand, he gestured toward the empty street in front of us, invoking an endless tangle of empty streets that lay further beyond. Just yesterday, he told me, he'd seen one sitting on the corner, waiting for a stoplight to turn green. *Yeah,* I said, *what's up with that?* But the truth was, I knew what he meant. The city was changing. Even the sky seemed new.

The closeness of things felt a little perverse. At the gym, as I ran on the treadmill, TV tuned to the aquarium channel, I'd stare past the screen and through the thick pane of glass and down into the pool where I'd first learned to swim. Sometimes I went on dates. Things would come out of my mouth and I'd think, *That sounds about right.* Everyone seemed to know something I didn't. The city was full of beautiful people. They crossed it in packs, luminescent, communicating. Money made their lives clean and mystical, gave them a dimension I could sense but not access. I wanted to hate them but didn't know how.

Some days, on my way to work, I rode the escalator through the biggest mall, never once stopping to look up at the geese. I could feel them there, hanging above me, drifting a little in the false air, keeping watch.

It turned out the study was in the same part of the university where I worked, but on the opposite side of the hall. Everything—chairs, fixtures, trick mirror—was the same, but pointed in the wrong direction. We all arranged our chairs into a circle. I stared at my knees so I wouldn't get seasick.

One by one, we introduced ourselves. The guy next to me told us he was an artist, that he had a "large colour vocabulary." Only one of the researchers wore a lab coat. It seemed somehow too small and too large at once, as if he'd let the hem out on a child's Halloween costume. Or stolen a real scientist's uniform and shrunk it in the wash.

Everyone was handed a clipboard with twenty blank pages attached. The researchers asked us to write as much as we could on the subject of colour—its purpose, how it functioned in our lives.

I took some time to think about it. The obvious strategy was to talk about nature or art, but I wanted to distinguish myself—to show that I understood the complex interplay between theory and the things it was designed to describe.[8] I pictured the researchers reading my response and was overcome by a wave of embarrassment so strong it felt almost sexual. I wondered how I could distance the person writing my answer from the one stranded inside it, forced to breathe in all its mistakes.

---

8   Several nights before, in the middle of an argument, a friend had put his hands on me, and put his mouth on mine, and grabbed a fistful of my hair and pulled until I pushed him off me. There seemed no graceful way to incorporate these facts into my response, but I couldn't keep them out; they'd see it on me, how invisible I was. I tried writing about lightning and lit cigarettes and trust, a trick that made your body disappear. Permission, presence, weakness. *Can't say no one warned you,* I wrote, and then crossed out, then wrote again.

I had some concerns about my eligibility. The researchers told me I was stereoblind, but decided that it would probably be okay. I typed the word into my phone:

In transitional moments, brief, unstable composites of two separate images may be seen, maintaining a contradictory tension. For example, vertical lines may appear, one at a time, to obscure horizontal lines from the left or from the right. Like a travelling wave, slowly switching one image for the other.

Once, I thought I had fallen in love with an artist who had built an organ you could play with your mind. It worked like this: you put on a headband that measured the nature and frequency of the electromagnetic waves emitted by your brain as you sat there and thought. These, in turn, triggered the instrument. The calmer you could get the lovelier the music became. *I think it's a joke about thinking too much,* he wrote to me.[9]

I'd wanted to try it so badly I thought I might drown. I watched the video a hundred times, memorized its warbling demonstration, up and down. But when I finally got the chance to play the organ in real life I couldn't make it sound like anything. Sitting in the middle of the gallery, headset sliding past my ears, I could not think a signal strong or calm enough. Still, later, writing to the artist, I told him it had sounded perfect, that it put the sprawling mess of me in order.

---

9   Sometimes I worried that a fundamental misunderstanding about the nature of the world was what made time do what it did to me. In moments of deep self-pity, I imagined the inside of my brain: the bright tangle of wires hanging loose at the ends, the spray of useless sparks when I tried to understand the distance between one thing and another.

The group got weird when we started discussing our answers; no one could agree about what *imaginary* meant, or even *possible*. We took a fifteen minute break.

Outside, I saw the artist. He was colourblind, he told me, but he wasn't going to tell them. He needed the money. Our breath rose up into the night, smoke trailed away from us in cursive, slower. He stamped his feet to keep blood moving through them. I asked what it was like to not see colour, and he said there was just one colour he couldn't see.

I asked if he'd tried to imagine what it looked like and he shrugged, looked me up and down again with fresh suspicion. I kept ending up in this conversation. *I guess the world gives you enough negative space,* I said. He nodded, wouldn't look at me.

The rooms were small. Each smelled like new plastic, cold metal, hairspray, fluorescent light. The researchers showed us the cameras and the mirrors. One of us volunteered to help with a demonstration. Before her, the screen flashed yellow first, then blue.

When my turn came, time moved like a record played back on top of itself. Alone, I went solid, drawn down to myself, the same size.

No one had told me what I was supposed to be seeing, or how long the experiment might last. I wondered whether this was art or science, or maybe just my fate's sum total: to sit still, waiting for someone to come tell me what I thought or saw or sounded like, what it meant. Sometimes I thought I could hear footsteps, or faint music coming in through the vents. Then I realized it was just the sound of water rushing through the pipes behind the walls.

Tape hiss, Value Village, vibraphones. On fixed-gears
scrubbed with salt and lemon, like the secret at the centre
of a Magic Eye the witches, genderless as light, breathe
green and lavender, appear and disappear, chanting your
passwords in a round. Voices like dimes dropped in a bowl,
blush ultraviolet, glittering auras. Skin so soft they move
through walls they press against your window, sing the
spell they wrote about the city there: *nothing belongs to you*
nothing belongs to you nothing belongs

The guy wants to know if he can prune his spruce himself;
he's worried about wind. *How big exactly is this tree?* asks
Ed, his cadence level, tone bemused. *I can't fit my arms
around it,* goes the guy. Which, look: kitchen table, chairs,
dog, sink, weak sunlight, radio, your front lawn in the
bruise and split of sunrise, kids and wife asleep. The spruce
predicting shadows in the driveway, how it croons and
keens against the night in the key of future, denting,
vantage, glass outside your bedroom. How insurance is a
prayer misfiring, how deep green makes your tongue taste
rust for weeks. How you can't but gaze into a pool of water,
Ed, without a spray of needles shattering the edges. How
the air can do you violence, speaking skips against the
present, reference fails and fails again. Maybe we have to
do it this way—voice and air and wires and distance. Trust.
Maybe the only metric is attempt: what can be held by you.
What you can stand to hold.

I liked going into the church. It all reminded me of
someone's childhood—how the woman dimmed the lights,
opened the door and brought the outside in, how we all lay
down, not touching, shoulders pressed against the
hardwood. *Float your ribcage,* she told us.[10] *Imagine two
globes inside you, spinning and spinning.*[11]

---

10   Above us, ceiling fans moved exactly the same way. Through
the high, clean, open windows, I heard children running in a
gymnasium—sneaker-echo weaving into searing pitch of *yes* and
no. Outside, in the hallway, I could hear a man yelling
instructions into his phone. Further off, the choir, singing.

11   Later, on my way home, I'd stand below and stare at
signage—like OSSINGTON TIRE with its lightning and time, or
GALAXY DONUTS with its galaxy—and think I'd failed my life so
often by assuming it had nothing left to teach me. In these
moments, I could see the other world that shimmered just below
the surface of this one. It was so close, I wondered why I couldn't
see it all the time.

You would know me if you saw me. I was late for everything and couldn't shake it, picked fights and felt certain each time. I squirmed in my chair at *I love you* and shrank from the light, could see my hand and touch you with my hand, but couldn't say whose hand it was. I was those blimps that hung out all day above the city in two kinds of weather, covered in tiny mirrors like a disco ball, complicating the sky. The only connection between me was this single, fraying signal. Above everything, I drifted, coming in and out and in and out and in.

At work, I watched a video of fifty men on graveyard shift at a factory. First something broke, then everybody ran toward it with their crowbars. Men fed whole trucks to a building-sized fire, and still it did not stop burning. *For example, a barge,* said the narrator, *can be melted all the way down to a single steel beam, or a hubcap.*

Some mornings, I'd wake up before you and just watch
your pulse float up against the thin skin of your throat. It
scared me. Sometimes I thought about your old car, the
one you had to leave for scrap outside of Montreal, that
carried you toward death and away from it. I didn't think it
would care to be reduced to metaphor. Sometimes I'd trace
the scar that ran from one side of your body to the other.
Could feel my blood turning liquid gold.

I kept having the same conversation. People watched me and I thought I saw the question pass between them as I spoke. I thought it might have to do with naming things, or death. What else? I pictured a machine. I said, *swallowing gravel*. I said *negative space, ownership, clean air, glass, both at the same time*. Still, it never worked the way I wanted. I wanted to write a poem with you in it, without time or apology, but I didn't know how. I was scared. *What else?* Downtown, men and women passed each other on the sidewalk. Everyone looked a little like my father. *Bright tangle of wires*, I thought among them, *screens, projector, joke about attention, the conventions of the instrument*. We all thought we knew each other from somewhere, but none of us could say for sure.

The church was exactly halfway between my house and the house I'd grown up in. Like always, we lay on our backs on the floor. The woman dimmed the lights. She asked us to imagine ourselves on a waterbed, or the surface of an endless sea, the blue-black waves arriving and retreating. We imagined ourselves small. We imagined a bicycle that just kept speeding up forever. We imagined ourselves on the overpass, holding hands and chanting. We could hear the choir. We remembered being children in the basement of the church, pounding on the table and screaming, eager to be allowed to begin.

I kept finding things under my pillow: brass unicorn, handful of crystals, a camera, etc. On my dresser, in a small dish shaped like a swan, was a single pill. Two perfect colours, a token from somebody's past. I didn't know if I could take it anymore. I wondered if this was a test.

I thought often of this email:

you're not lying but it seems like you're omitting things. it's like saying an avalanche isn't about snow, it's about temperature and gravity and vibrations or whatever

Sometimes, alone in the grocery store, I felt hands in my hair or on my shoulders. For a second I'd just stand there, tiny and breathing in tape hiss, lifted out of me and stuttering, stuck between this channel and the next. *It takes a lot of work,* the narrator tells us, *to turn one enormous thing into a small part of another. It takes heat and dust and force and time.*

At first I thought we were talking about gesture, that you didn't know what it was like to be pinned down. *It's a movie,* I said. In this scene, it's 4 a.m. A woman is lying on her back in the wet grass, refusing to get up, no matter how you ask her. Or she's waiting in the bar for a narrator who won't co-operate. Or she's sleeping in the back of a van with her friend at the wheel. Or she's standing on the street while you rush by her without saying a thing, or she's tripping down the rotting stairs of her apartment, or she's crushed against the wall and scaring you, her mouth a doorway to another world.

I said that in the poem I was teaching you a lesson, that I had to, that it was my job.

Still, I could feel the real argument shimmering under this one, see it move. You said, *I like when it's brought up, remembered, made real.* You said, *so much of it feels like it happened to somebody else, or in a parallel life, decoupled from this.* You said, *I'm scared of it dissolving into not-me anymore.* You said that pain works this way too, can be a bridge or split the signal for a second, lets this near-forgotten thing return to where it came from, where it perhaps belongs.

Carlo, (I didn't say) I'm sorry that I laugh sometimes when you see the ghost of your old car in parking lots, about the whole thing with your name and how I don't know how to put it in the poem without making it about me too, about the past and future, how they skip inside the present. I think you make me feel like I belong inside my body, and I think I'm scared to call things what they are. You said *something that is yours but not of you, two arrows splitting off and pointing back to the same place, together.* Like a palindrome (I said), and you said no, like something else entirely.

Later, on my way home or back from it, or in the church, alone with everyone, I moved all the way through me like light through a prism. The windows were open. First the choir came in, then my childhood, then the signal, the sound of a streetcar, your voice: all parts of the same chord that held itself against itself, refusing to resolve. Outside, at the edges of this world, I could feel the real one waiting. I felt new, or something like it. I felt new.

NOTES

N12 In the province of Ontario, an N12 form is also known as a "Notice to End Your Tenancy Because the Landlord, a Purchaser or a Family Member Requires the Rental Unit." The Ontario Place project in the poem is based on the *in/future* art festival, which took place there in 2016. The description of "typical tree behaviour" is taken from the wall text for Robert Hengeveld's "SSSpun." The song from the mixtape is "I'm His Child" by Sister Ernestine Washington.

Yes and No This poem was written in a bygone era when "Like" and "Nope" were the only two directions you could swipe on Tinder.

Voight-Kampff and *ESPER* are two pieces of fictional technology from the movie *Blade Runner.* Voight-Kampff machines help determine whether a subject is human or a replicant by measuring their involuntary reactions—like pupil dilation and EEG waves—during a test "designed to provoke an emotional response." ESPER machines let you move through two-dimensional photographs like they're three-dimensional scenes. The poem "ESPER" also cribs a couple of lines from Frank Bidart's "Borges and I."

Impossible Colour Stereoblindness is the inability to percieve depth. The quote about it comes from the Wikipedia page for "Binocular Rivalry." The study in this poem is (very loosely) based on (my very amateur understanding of) research conducted by Hewitt Crane and Thomas Piantanida in 1983, where participants were asked to stare at two-colour patterns with one eye covered until the areas of their brains that percieved the colours as separate were "overridden." Some participants claimed they could see a completely new colour that didn't exist in the normal visible spectrum. Some of those said they kept seeing it long after the experiment was over. The mind-reading organ is based on a piece of art by Craig Fahner called "Organ." ("Here and Now" and "Begin with the End in Mind" both borrow three-quarters of a phrase from the artist's statement for this project.) Coyotes, like all dogs, can't tell the difference between red and green.

The first poem in the book is for Alison Lawrence.
"N12" is for Layne Hinton, Bronwen Doran, Sam Lewis, and Levi.
"Begin with the End in Mind" is for Carlo Spidla.

ACKNOWLEDGEMENTS

This book exists because of grants from the Toronto Arts Council, the Ontario Arts Council, and the Canada Council for the Arts. They gave me time to write when I had none, and I'm extremely grateful for it.

A couple of the poems in this book appeared, ages ago, in *The Hairpin* and *Post Road Magazine*. Thanks to the editors of those publications—in particular Haley Mlotek, who doubles as wonderful friend.

I owe a great deal to Damian Rogers (who is real magic) for her kindness and support, to Gil Adamson for her copyediting, and to everyone at Anansi for their work.

This book belongs, in different ways, to my parents and my grandmother. Jack Gross and Tess Edmonson provided the birthday party, couch, and spell of calm where I wrote the parts I like best. Yanyi gave characteristically brilliant advice near the end. Paul Saulnier is important. Mike Chaulk is a forever friend. Endless love and gratitude to all pals, but especially Deragh Campbell, Dorothea Paas, Layne Hinton, and Sarah Ford, who talk with me about everything all the time.

Thanks especially to Kevin Connolly, the most thoughtful, generous, and patient editor I've ever had the pleasure of working with.

& finally, thank you to Carlo Spidla, who makes the world bigger.

97

EMMA HEALEY's first book of poems, *Begin with the End in Mind*, was published by ARP Books in 2012. Her poems and essays have been featured in places like the *Los Angeles Review of Books*, the FADER, the *Hairpin*, *Real Life*, the *National Post*, the *Globe and Mail*, the *Toronto Star*, the *Walrus*, *Toronto Life*, and *Canadian Art*. She was poetry critic at the *Globe and Mail* and is a regular contributor to the music blog *Said the Gramophone*. She was the recipient of the Irving Layton Award for Creative Writing in both 2010 and 2013, a National Magazine Award nominee in 2015, and a finalist for the K.M. Hunter award in 2016.